GIRL WITH A RING IN HER HEART

KAVERI GOGOI

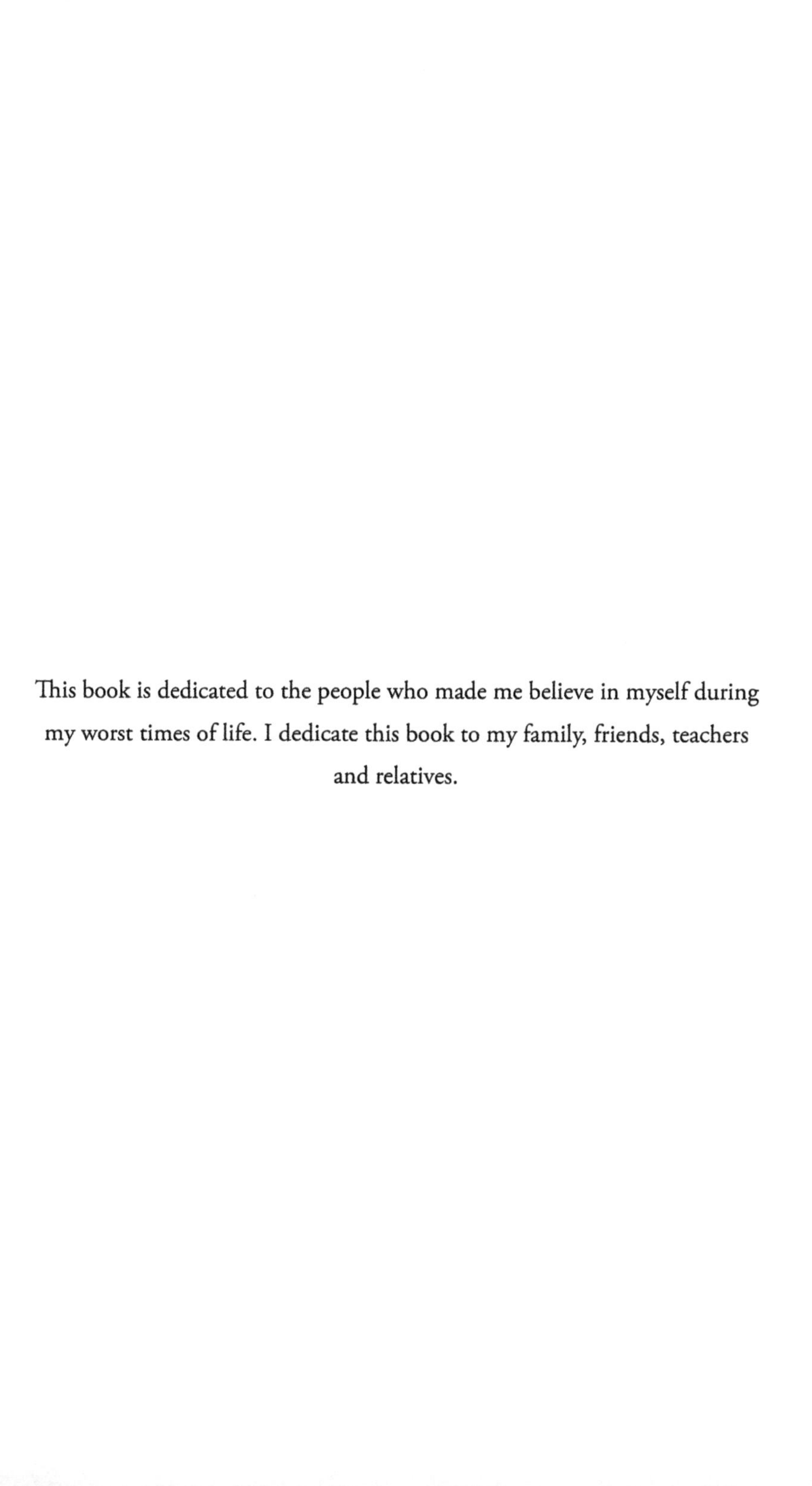

This book is dedicated to the people who made me believe in myself during my worst times of life. I dedicate this book to my family, friends, teachers and relatives.

Contents

Contents

Preface

The poems written in this book are mostly self experienced while others are brought from imagination. It is said that love is the best feeling in this world. It indeed is. I have been a lover too at times. At other times, when I was not a lover in action, I was a writer pouring my heart out in words with ink on paper or some other ways.

Acknowledgements

Deepest thanks to my many patient, generous, and helpful readers. I would like to thank the people who came and stayed in my life. I would pay my love and respect to my family, teachers and relatives for their endless support. I want to mention my dearest friends Fatima and Aparupa who helped me so much while editing my poems. I also want to thank my other friends who have always loved me and supported me in my journey of life. I want to tell them that I am so less without them and I spread my wings of love towards them.

Prologue

There are few people who find final love at first or second hand. Whereas there are people like me and you who touch many shadows till the end of our lives to either to ruin or spread love. However, none of us end up simply. People from each groups writes their heart out in poems and stories to share their happiness and miseries. Each one has a different and unique beginning as well as ending. This book is about first love, lost love, heartbreak, falling in love again and the process continues. The writer hopes that the process begins to take a new turn one day and hopes for the best.

1. Hometown

Last three Christmas I spent my time with you.
But this Christmas, you found someone new.
Lately I have been becoming a mess and
thinking of ways to get up from bed.
I have also been thinking about a lot of boys.
Maybe my momma knows that, as I make some noises.
As the cold is not going either.
Would you want me back as your partner?
I can surely live without you
but cannot be the thunder.
Grab a beer, grab my back.
I will give you everything this time without thinking of a hack.
And the rain is getting heavier.
I can't stop by your house now.
Will you come and join me in my simple home town?

2. Young

Just remember what I said as you give up another chance on our dreams.
People may notice only the mole on your face.
But the body says more, more than any tongue could ever explore.
So baby, touch me tonight and make me whole of yours.
Forever and ever and ever more.
We would drink glasses of wine in the bath tub.
The crowds wouldn't matter anything to us, like it did some other nights.
I will play the brave young girl,
running away from home to live my dreams of dancing.
You will be fine living with your friends upstairs.
But would you hold my hands and not miss the chance
of letting us go again like we did in our past lives.
Our secret memories laid behind and only known to us,
as they couldn't see, they couldn't breathe the love affair of two young birds.

3. The boy I loved the most

The same old story has been told through several poems.
I have a thing for nostalgia.
Living in the 90s era, where love sounded like some truth and felt like magic booth.
Damn, I thought he was a fool because he was really not at school.
But he has been the player and makes everything he wears look so cool.
Six missed calls and yet not called me back.
But he told me that he would have loved me as his better half.
Random girls I heard sleep in your bed.
Doing dirty little things and kisses in your forehead.
I hate the fact is the way you mocked me when I said it was
easier to travel with books rather than chicks on your chest.
I know you were once a best friend.
But all that you have done to me gives you the worst friend tag ever.
All those big love games and short tempered tantrums that I am not used to, don't show me that.

4. Cold weather

A cozy place we have found for all of us,
where bonfire and dim lights would do
justice to our friendships in this cold weather.
We would sit down on the ground with
guitars on our hands and songs in our lips.
This winter is going to be magical and just
as we planned five years ago when we were seventeen.
Most of us are now like the cold weather itself,
calm and pleasant.
I wish we would have known our personality traits
at the time we planned this cool trip.
Some of us are couples since standard twelve amongst
ourselves while others are planning to get married to aliens
in the next five to seven years.
However, this bond shall always remain.
We will never forget this cold weather and the hot tea
from Assam with some crispy fries made of the things we like.

5. New love

Found new love,
In the midst of rush and hush.
Never thought I could ruin and love myself so much at the same time.
The air smelled a bit pleasant.
Freedom and independence were the new rules.
The cold felt like I could be the most passionate with
that one person I thought to be mine, who thought of me to be his.
New dating patterns, new kisses on the lips,
holding on to each other no matter what happened.
Breaths were heavier as he came close by although love was all in the air.
I gave thousand expressions when he looked at me.
I gave him millions of smiles and he pictures them in his heart.
What he gave me was a bit of messy thing to understand at first.
But when he fell boldly in love, I knew he was mine.
Now I find his clothes on my bed and arms on my chest.
And even if the society thinks it's too young an age,
We tell them that it's too young an age not to fall and get up for one another.

6. Memories bring back to you

Remember when we first met in ninth grade?
We were passing notes from the teacher's desk.
You were looking at me with those golden eyeballs and I couldn't speak a word to you.
Maybe not being brave was a trait of mine then but I promise that's not me today.
While it's been a long time I met you.
You are still stuck on my head as if I am studying your teenage traits.
There's always a relief in sharing secrets through poems to the readers and
who will know it better than you.
A friend of mine just told that I am an old soul staying on a Generation Z's body.
Your voice while reciting those three lines of your first poem, I still remember that.
Also my heart just gets magnified to the core when I recall you smiling broadly at me with your dimples.
I just want us to meet somewhere where we can get lost in our thoughts
and share kisses under the old blue sky.
Till then I will visit you through the memories I have kept in my life's memory.

7. Lust affairs

You said clearly in your mind "I don't have time for the foreplay.
Let me play it like my other rituals."
I was blinded by the lights of innocence.
Had a hundred, thousand words written by you on trying
to prove a point that can be better understood by you.
I have been tired of these silly circles of crazy lust affairs.
Erase the memory that we were talking about our future.
I hope to share the story to my friends and lovers that you
don't get the girl by taking her below her status.
Fear isn't in my head now because my momma told me not to
trust the ones who are hungry wolves of lust affairs.

8. Undo the love for you

You should know I did that,
I covered my hands with gloves.
Although wanted to wear my heart on my sleeves,
but I was afraid to, that you would pinch it and blow it to hell.
But right now, I am in heaven looking at you shorter than my breath,
forgiving you taller than your height,
listening to your lies and throwing them in the dirt.
What a mysterious thing for me, that I would forget you like that,
Undo the love kept for you and take it to someone else.
He just loves the smile on my face.
Also cares when he brings tears to my round face.
He is not like you.
Yeah not even a bit.
He kisses me like cherries in the sunshine,
last sip in the bottle of red wine. He is not like you.
Yeah! Not a bit.
He shares his deepest secrets by singing them through his melodious voice.
He does everything you didn't do but you needed to.
He touches every part of my soul and I can't stop but fix my broken heart with glue.

9. Guess it's getting worse

I am losing my self control.
Would you forgive me for my small mistakes?
Ten days in heaven but then I couldn't believe myself
that I could be happy and lovely with someone else.
Then you gave me that sound, bitter which I didn't want.
Thought I should better run and find myself escapism
by turning off like no one else around.
Guess you shouldn't have been this bitter.
Listened to my tongue tied words, tackled with my troubles.
Maybe it could have made it easier.
I don't want to break it but if we break it, I am thinking of running away.
I will run away far from all this rapport and highs.
I will have to bring that towel which had really soaked my
preceding rain from the color of the eyes that you once liked.
Guess it's getting even worse.
Thinking how I would deal with these small fights and thinking
how I would cross the scars of two people getting older.
It's these complexes that I hate.
Maybe we are in love, maybe we are not.
But guess it's really getting worse.

10. Take me with you

Take me for a movie, take me for a drink.
Then take me for a bike ride with your pride that I am sitting next to you.
Show me the sunsets, show me stars and
show me the scars that you have got in your arms.
Red wine, oranges and few books on our backpacks;
we are ready to go to be the real marvels.
Picnics in early dinosaurs spots,
adventures of different kinds and most of all
what you are yearning for at this time.

11. What am I now?

I cry like the longest river during rainy days sometimes.
I also laugh like seeing a joker in the middle of a ghostly scene.
I am a human with some robotic dreams.
But each day when I try to plan my day, the day plans me.
I love my friends and their hearts they carry within.
I run to temples and pray for them even when I am sick.
But skipped visiting the temple that day and made love to you instead.
God knows what was written on my bones and skin that were made old in the process.
My friends get angry when I tell them the truth.
I heard they have insecurities that are controlling their mouth.
They blame me for being rude sometimes.
But there's a scar on my heart too, which gets heavy at times.

12. Run away

Ran away each time I seemed to look small.
But this time I have confessed someone and stood tall.
Although got ignored and faced one or two big empty halls.
Still the reward is of no waste at all.
The reward is finding me every time I fall.
Every time I go around and try to at least crawl.
I do want to know you baby, I really want to do.
Despite your big reputation of being a sugar boo.
My heart beat is getting faster than ever before.
I don't know if I should stop here or go to the shore.
I have been counting pennies in my pocket to go to the zoo.
Should I wait for you or run away like each time I do?

13. Love me like you did

I miss you silently in the crowd.

I miss you suddenly in the dark.

I have loved and lost people so far from the time you are gone.

And you, you are like the stars in the sky, shining brightly but not there beside.

I want to be loved, like I used to be.

I also want to love, like before.

Just as pure like it used to be.

I want you in the middle of the woods or in the house.

I want to live with you and love you like back then.

I want you near me, baby.

Don't run away this time.

Don't you think I am crazy.

I am just like a glass of wine.

14. Drowned

Since, I was done with fire,
I thought I will play with the rain
And live happily in the lake.
He told me to choose the ocean full of love.
But the contemplation went reverse.
Suddenly, I saw only the perils.
He was nowhere to be found.
I guess I was just drowned,
in a pocket full of warmth.
Took seriously what was to be taken with funny names.
And do you know now where he points all the blame?
He says "It's not you, it's just me trying to play some cool games.
So don't ruin my life by narrating this story to me again and again."
I cried more than few buckets full of tears from
all the pain that I have gathered in years.
It sucks to tell you that the one who tried to bow back
one's affection to him was shot in the head.
Tried calling doctors from all over the place and have found
people laughing at me whom I once called peers.

15. Maybe

Now you look at her, the way you looked at me.
Right now, you might be kissing in the dark.
And during the day, guessing each other's birth month through the sunrays.
Yes, I met her thrice.
She looks so beautiful.
I talked to her twice.
She seems so smart.
I know she is talented too.
Maybe I am jealous of her.
And it reminds me of you and
the way we left because somebody interfered.
I thought I would never love you but as I look
at you in the middle of the streets with her now,
I can't help but think about you.
I miss the chances of what if we would stay together.
You would play the guitar and sing sweet songs for me.
I would mesmerize you the way everybody talks with me.
Your brother, your sister, your aunts, those who love you
to the moon and the stars used to tell me I was deserving of the status.

16. Souls speaking in the night

The writers will be bleeding on their paper when the night cries.
The heartbreakers will be tearing their pillows apart when the night arrives.
I will be dancing to the legacy of the stars that shines in the night sky.
You will be talking to the moon about the conversation that took place at
the dinner table with your broken family.
Half dead, half asleep.
We belong to the same company, manifesting our inner demons
to the same audience, again and again.
You know better now how to shout and say my name out loud.
I know better how to make actions speak louder than words now.
Let's move to the sink, vomit all our hate we created in our minds.
Let's move to the typewriter and bleed all the love found in our souls.
Let's make our thoughts move to cities and countries we have never been.
Let's talk to people those we have never seen.
Let's make this world better now.

17. Dirty little things

You like my hips and I like your lips in a sensual way.
I will touch your body more than anyone has ever loved it baby.
I will love your soul more than I love poetry itself.
Honey, you have known me within a count of three.
There is a familiar vibe I get from you that I get from the flowers that bloom.
I know you will set the stories of me doing the studious things apart and love me till I bloom as well.
Will you marry me with watches instead of tiny rings?
I will mind my time with you instead of staring at shiny things.
I know you will take me home with all your dirtiest jokes saved for me.
Baby, how have I been so lucky to be with you even?

18. Falling and rising

I was hoping that I wasn't the only one falling in love with the most special one in my life.
I was praying that I could be able to trust someone and start over again.
Would you fall in love with me?
Would you sing the songs you heard when all else were talking shit about me?
All those who were slut shaming people like me are giving five divorces in a year now.
All those who talked about finding the only one in life are struggling to even find themselves somehow.
So will you be my sunshine in a rainy day?
We shall walk over the green grasses on our way.
We shall click pictures on mountain tops after climbing all our way.
We will be jumping together from the mountain tops to the sea.
Will you stare at me with those magical eyes over and over again?

19. Never clearly understood

I was taking all these swings and you were on the mood.
I could land up with alluring things but I was somewhere on the road.
Now I am clear about my goals but I am afraid of being called rude
while dressing up as honeybees have always been my route.
I am wearing a little green which will uplift up my whole mood.
I have been writing all these stuffs which will never be clearly understood.
You were quite the vulture ripping all the culture.
I was grouping all the cool ones.
For them it was a bombshell to find you there.
I saw you smirking at the idiots.
They saw you chilling with the fools.
I guess a few tiny little cuts have detached your body from your soul.
Maybe a demon snapped your mind and exchanged it with yours.

20. Disappear

I am not going to love anyone else for a week or a month.

Because every time I love somebody, I get disconnected so easily.

I am just dying to love myself now.

Mysteriously disappear from thedaylights.

Hide in the center of the world in the dark nights.

Whisper some voices to myself when spotted in hell through the map.

Heaven is for marigolds and Godlike creatures, unlike me.

I am nowhere close to that because I have broken some hearts and some future families.

Took their intolerance and gave birth of many.

I was also a prey of just his prettiness.

Don't tell me to even make him a mess.

I just clearly want to run away in the wild again.

Top quality music playing on my brain.

Extraordinary marks have been attached on my body.

Maybe somebody attacked me, while I was in deep sleep.

There is no perfect place to stay when I am not in the mood for loving somebody in their way.

There is handful of lousy memories still tingling on my brain.

What makes me ecstatic gets swept off in the rain.

21. Your fame, your name

Kissing in the terrace and having it after marriage was my cup of tea that you destroyed.
Still, I look at you and I don't even hate you.
I just wonder why I wasn't afraid to lose you.
Now maybe karma's taking scream.
I don't even dream about you, like I dreamt of him.
Maybe it's a little confusing for you.
I also can tell you are not getting it.
So I infer some insights to you.
I told you I wasn't ready to do what you do to too many girls in a row.
I was just teasing you to make a bed and a pillow.
You took off the bedsheet, wrapped it underneath my body.
Soft little kisses were what all I needed.
I told you to not cross the line at once.
But honey, you are lame.
You thought me as a game.
You wondered about your fame.
So I left you saying goodbye to your name.

22. Revenge

Some friends told me I was obsessed when I was only upset.
My best friend told them it was just a phase.
All you knew was that I cried in buckets or roads filled with drains.
I never tell lies. So, darling today it's time for you to hurry up in your own race.
Now I change my clothes as you change your colors.
I clear my throat and all I do is roar.
Teach some humble lessons to your innocent buyers.
Throw my diary in a guzzling fire.
Put a whistle on my mouth and hold a gun on my hand.
Remove devils like you from my beloved mother land.
Some call me strange and others call me brave.
But one day you will surely know the meaning of crave.
East or the west side, beauty lies inside.
What lies outside is your tongue that sucks from all sides.

23. Dream of you

I saw you in my dreams.
We were so young again,
I was born out of love and pain.
You were giving lectures in board meetings.
I was waiting for you in the hope of spring, in a man's mind.
You were tolerating my numerous phone calls, repetitive in the way your phone rings.
I was asking thousand questions in my mind, if not less of where and how you could be.
I saw my friends passing by.
I thought to myself if I could cry.
But they would ask unsolicited questions which will go in vain.
What would I gain?
So I kept my doubts to myself and rang your phone again.
This time I could see you running towards me, with a bouquet of flowers and showers of rain.

24. Me and this generation

There are cameras flashing all over my face during this time of the hours.

They make even my nervous system anxious.

I kept on making notes of hopes and pleasures.

That one day I will find in that dining table of ours.

I shall take a look of your eyes and capture them in my heart's pores.

And wait for the wild animal in my body that roars.

I felt like caged love birds changing my appearance all the time to grab your attention.

But I have to mention about the valuable lessons I got from all the rejections.

I don't have much regrets but I feel like someone old to this generation.

Or else why would they put me in this regular mode of detention?

Hope my parents don't have any tensions and questions regarding my occupation.

Cause they saw me dancing in a very big mansion,

although I might have forgotten to tell them about my new job and profession.

25. Befriend me

I got hundreds of problems and titles of my bad records
But I am still smiling at the cameras for posters and better home decors.
I wish I had alien on the middle of my name because
I feel like a pillion on the bike rides and the middle-east game.
As I was clueless and standing in the middle of a field,
I couldn't recognize any lyrics of the song that he sang as his shield.
Getting my stories told even after ages by strangers
And the friend who caused the fire became enemy.
Dancing beside the lake,
Giving you too many handshakes
Days I have gone through
that you have never got a clue.

9 798886 842470

Printed by Libri Plureos GmbH in Hamburg, Germany